BEYOND
the Woes of Me!

McDougal & Associates
Servants of Christ and Stewards of the
Mysteries of God

BEYOND
the Woes of Me!

By

Dr. Dawn Greay

Published by:
McDougal & Associates
18896 Greenwell Springs Road
Greenwell Springs, LA 70739
www.ThePublishedWord.com

McDougal & Associates is dedicated to the spreading of the Gospel of Jesus
Christ to as many people as possible in the shortest time possible.

ISBN 978-1-950398-57-7

Printed on demand in the US, the UK, Australia and the UAE
For Worldwide Distribution

Dedication

My motivation for all that I do starts and ends with my kids. Each has been instrumental in some way, encouraging me to propel as high as the sky. To the memory of Eric, to Courtney, Jerrell, Danisha, Rhea, and Malcolm—all my heartbeats. It is love given and reciprocated that helps me to release this book.

*Whoever dwells in the shelter of the Most High
will rest in the shadow of the Almighty.
I will say of the LORD, "He is my refuge and my
fortress, my God, in whom I trust."*
— Psalm 91:1-2

*Cast all your anxiety on him
because he cares for you.*
— 1 Peter 5:7

Contents

Foreword by Evangelist Sharon M. Billy

You will show me the path of life; in Your presence is fullness of joy, at Your right hand there are pleasures forevermore.
Psalm 16:11, AMPC

As I read and meditated on the poems in *Beyond the Woes of ME,* it seemed as if Dr./Elder Dawn was allowed to pull back the curtains of our very own life's journey and was given the privilege to have a glance at both our highs and lows. She has captured the very essence of the *woes* and beyond of life from the very beginning, starting with Section One "Don't Quit," to Section Three "Finding Me," and concluding with Section Four, "Finding God."

Foreword by Evangelist Sharon M. Billy

In this book, you will discover that despite the woes, there is a place of new chapters in life, and the next and so on, never giving up and never just simply "throwing in the towel!" Her words bring you to a resting place, knowing that it's the Almighty who is leading you in a maze with such beautiful threads of tapestry too complicated for mere man to unwind. But, when we stop, breathe and rest, what fullness of joy we find in His presence! It is here as Dr./Elder Dawn takes us to "Made Whole" and reminds us that we are "More Than a Conqueror" and yes, "Chosen!"

This is a must-read book of poems, always in season, and most certainly, a ministry tool with which to bless others.

I thank the Almighty for you and am always in remembrance of you in my prayers.

Evangelist Sharon M. Billy

Foreword by Anita W. Dennis

Dr. Dawn Greay is a phenomenal woman of God. In this book, *Beyond the Woes of Me*, she utilizes poetic expressions to paint vivid images of her observations, exposures, and experiences while navigating life from adolescence to adulthood. Her words candidly show how God loves and blesses His children, enabling us to persevere despite life's challenges. Dr. Greay utilizes biblical scriptures to remind us of this and to inspire, to encourage, and to show us that there is always *HOPE!*

Anita W. Dennis,
Retired Educator and Author

Foreword by LaTescia Parnell

I am a long-time friend of Dr. Dawn Greay and am very proud to call her Sister and Friend. As I read her book, *Beyond the Woes of Me*, I was overcome with so many emotions. This is her life story written in poems. I have watched Dr. Dawn overcome many adversities in life through worship.

This book will inspire you to never give up HOPE. The answer is on the way. The book will also remind ladies all over the world that we are uniquely created by God.

LaTescia Parnell

Introduction

Beyond the Woes of ME is a compilation of poems written while I traveled the road of life. As a teenager, experiencing the highs and lows of life and with no other outlet, I began to put my feelings on paper. Throughout my life, the thoughts and journaling of words continued, and thus a blessing from the Lord came about to inspire, to encourage, and simply to give HOPE to others. Through it all, I have learned to put my trust in God.

Dawn Greay

Section 1

Don't Quit

He Will Show You the Way

You feel there is no way.
You just can't make it through another day.
How can you see what lies ahead?
With every step you take,
you feel only dread.

But you can hold your head up now,
For my God will show you how
To see the steps along the way.
They get brighter and better, day by day.

Draw nigh to Him daily, as you pray.
Often, lips are speechless,
Words you just can't find to say.
Yet you feel His hands of love,

He Will Show You the Way

As He comforts and sends
Strength from above.
Though tired and weary
Your mind may be,
He gives you peace and sweet relief.
Come, sit my child! Lie here! Just rest!
I gave My love.
I gave My best.

Always Wrong

No matter what I do
No matter what I say
Everything done and said is
Just the wrong way.

I try so hard to keep pressing on.
All of my hopes and dreams
Will soon be gone.

Somebody, can you please tell me:
What's really going on?
Because everything I do and say
Seems to always be wrong.

When Death Knocks at Your Door

Do you know how it feels
Living in misery and strife?
It's so hard when you find out
A loved one took their own life.

At first, when you see them,
The person appears to be glad.
Then, the next few days, they seem so sad.
Instead of facing their problems,
They take what they consider
The easy way out.
Because they did one wrong thing,
They think it's over.
Yet, no one knows what it's all about.

Beyond the Woes of Me!

"Why did they do it?"
That's what others say.
"I can't believe it."
Yet, they're gone away.
This can't be true. It's just a dream.
You face reality. Then you scream.
"I loved them so. How could this be?
Why did this have to happen
In my reality?"
Express your love for them
While they are here.
Then, when they are gone,
Their presence you will feel so near.

Many times they tried to tell you
What was going on.
They tried to say, "I need your help."
But you just left them alone.

Is it really all their fault?
They tried to get help from you.

However, you didn't recognize their pain.
It would not sink through.
So, help them when they knock.
Answer when they call.

Everyone needs help from time to time.
For no one can do it all.

Get rid of the misery.
Get rid of the strife.
Pray and ask God
To come into your life.

Reality

Sure, it's easy to say, "I'm tired of this.
I can't take it anymore."
It's easy to throw in the towel
And head straight for the door.

You know it's even easy
To proclaim what it could be.
But who wants to deal with reality?

So, in running from what is
And heading to what shall be,
We hope, we dream, we watch, we wait,
But still, some of us escape reality.

Many days come, and the nights they go.
Still, we persevere and challenge
our gravest foe—
REALITY.

Not Time to Die

The lives of the children are in limbo.
The hearts of the same are waxing cold.
In a world of complacency,
The answer is not in you or me.

For we must turn from our own way
Through God and His mercy.
His love is everlasting.
The truth is His Word.
His voice can be heard.

Cry out for the young man
Who can be changed.
For it's not their time to die.

Know that salvation is for all.
So is life ... until you're called.
Don't let them slip into the pit to fall.

Beyond the Woes of Me!

Let them know God is in control.
He can give peace
To their troubled souls.
It's not their time to die.

Who will stand for them to fight?
Let them know the ways that are right.

Who will show them
The way of God's love?
The kind you get only from Above.

Who will let them know
It's not time to die?

Life is given to all.
Choose to live!
Choose to give!
Choose to love!

IT'S NOT TIME TO DIE, YOUNG PEOPLE!

The Youth

Many people think
The youth have so little to say.
Many people think
They have nothing to do.
Well, there is much the youth must say.
There is also much work for them to do.

Amid it all, many will go astray.
But a gentle reminder to all:
There are so many of our youth
Who will follow through.

The youth are the future, and guess what?
It's not that far away.
They are the ones who will hold tomorrow.
They must be the ones
Who will live it today.

Scriptures on HOPE

So the poor have hope,
and injustice shuts its mouth.
— Job 5:16

Do you have eyes of flesh?
Do you see as mortal sees?
— Job 10:4

I rise before dawn and cry for help;
I have put my hope in your word.
— Psalm 119:147

"For I know the plans I have for
you," declares the LORD, "plans to
prosper you and not to harm you,
plans to give you hope and a future."
— Jeremiah 29:11

For in this hope we were saved. But
hope that is seen is no hope at all. Who
hopes for what they already have?
— Romans 8:24

Your Notes

Section 2

Finding Love

All About Love

Love is something two people share,
Showing their feelings
And how much they care.

It may be a relative, a friend, or a lover.
In this game we call life,
It's important to share
Our love with others.

It's a special feeling that's deep inside.
It hides within the heart,
But it comes out in vibes.

It's a choice we make to be selfless,
To give, to share, and to support
Whatever the need may be.

All About Love

It's a compromise to give, to take,
And to trust for eternity.

Though it's a great feeling
From the heart so true,
It's often difficult to say
The words "I Love You."

As you sit there and wonder
What words to choose.
Don't put it off until tomorrow.
Find the right words to use.

Sometimes you wait and take too long.
Please don't let that be you.
The love you have may soon be gone.
Then, what's left for you to do?

Find the time, speak the words,
And let your actions show.
You really love the people in your life,
And you should want each of them
To know.

Love for Mother

I couldn't find the right words to say.
Yet, I couldn't express
My feelings another way.

But there is something I want you to know
Before either of us must go.

What I have to say is true.
To my mother: I LOVE YOU!

This comes from within my heart.
This had to be said
Before either of us departs.
Mom, I Love You!

Little Kid

Little kid, little kid, what are you saying?
Are you going inside now,
Or are you still playing?
I'm going to talk to my momma.
Gotta let her know I love her.

By Malcolm Jr.
(5th grade)

Daydream

There's a thought.
There's a dream.
It was like a nightmare,
And I just wanted to scream.
When I blink my eyes now, it's gone.
Wow! What a daydream!
Gone! Gone! Gone!

Oh, yet again comes the smile
That has come upon my face.
There it is again, my great daydream,
Back in its rightful place.

The love,
The bliss,
The wonderful kiss

Daydream

Of God's great sunshine as
it touches my face.
Daydreaming and thinking
About His amazing grace.

My First Love

It's funny how time can change.
For people change too.
I know that I can say
I once really loved you.

I hope you understand
What I'm trying to say.
For I never thought
That my love would go away.

So many times I opened my heart.
But there was always
Something in the way,
Something, it felt like this huge block
That wouldn't go away.

My First Love

After you, I will never be the same.
My attitudes toward love and life,
Yes, I say, they have changed.

Even though we're friends,
Both pretending not to know,
Those around us could tell,
Why?
Our eyes, our touch, our smile,
Our laugh, our conversation.
Through it all, our love did show.

You're Special to Me

You are my friend,
One who is so dear.
Whenever I need you,
You are always near.

I shed a tear.
You wiped it dry.
If it wasn't for God and you,
All I would ever do is cry.

You comfort me, love me,
And make me feel secure.
I know there's love within your heart.
A love that's rare and pure.

The love of a friend that I know
Was sent from God above,
To speak new life

You're Special to Me

And words of HOPE,
And to show the Father's love.

You make me feel so fine.
You make me feel so wanted,
As if you were all mine.

My heart is all for you right now,
Because I'm feeling low.
I could take the memories we share
And walk straight out the door.

My heart is sometimes melting.
I feel sorry for myself.
I'm like an unread book,
Just sitting on the shelf.

It seems I'm the only reason
They are still together.
I wish I wasn't even around.
Maybe things would be much better.

Beyond the Woes of Me!

I should be happy.
Writing poetry brings me cheer.
When I think of life's challenges,
My eyes fill with tears.

There were times when I had problems.
You spoke words that made me feel good.
I love you, my friend, with all my heart,
Just like any good friend should.

Just know: you are my special friend!

The Two of Us

The two of us it's going to be,
Walking hand in hand.
I will by your woman;
You will be my man.

The two of us it's going to be.
On that exciting day,
We will say our vows,
And place our wedding rings.
Then together, we'll walk away.

The two of us it's going to be.
For it will be forevermore.
We've shown the world all our love.
Now it's something others want to explore.

Beyond the Woes of Me!

It's a great feeling that we have.
It's like a dream come true.
Everything that I do
I want to do with you.

God Gives

Sometimes you feel there is no way.
You just can't make it through another day.

With every step you take, you dread.
You have a broken heart.
You have a bowed down head.

But you can hold your head up now.
Our Father God will show you how.
Let Him lead you along the pathway.
Which gets brighter, better every day.

Draw nigh to Him daily as you pray.
Often your lips are speechless
And words you just can't find to say.

Beyond the Woes of Me!

Yet, you feel His hands of love.
He guides you through life.
His Word, it gives you hope.
He comforts you and sends
Strength from above.
Though tired and weary
Your mind may be.
Know that He gives peace and sweet relief.

Come, sit, my child! Lie here and rest!
I gave you My love.
I gave you My best.

*For God so loved the world that he gave his one
and only Son, that whoever believes in him shall
not perish but have eternal life.*
—John 3:16

Scriptures on LOVE

Give thanks to the God of gods.
His love endures forever.
— Psalm 136:2

Love the Lord your God with
all your heart and with all your
soul and with all your mind
and with all your strength.
— Mark 12:30

But God demonstrates his own
love for us in this: While we were
still sinners, Christ died for us.
— Romans 5:8

But because of his great love for us,
God, who is rich in mercy, made
us alive with Christ even when we
were dead in transgression—it is
by grace you have been saved.
— Ephesians 2:4-5

Your Notes

Section 3

Finding Me

Bye, High School

This is the end of high school for me.
I guess you could say that I'm happy.
Then, on the other hand, I'm not so happy.

I'll be saying goodbye
To all my friends and some enemies.
I guess I'll be making
New friends and enemies elsewhere.
I'll be living for today
And not tomorrow, nor yesterday.

Yes, there will be lots of memories
Of lots of loves,
But the future holds but one for me.

Bye, High School

Maybe it will be happiness
Filled with bliss.
I hope not too much sorrow or gloom.
I'll just take a break,
Stop, and reminisce.

I'll just try to do my best
In whatever it is I do.
Maybe college, maybe work.
Of that, right now, I don't know.
But bye to high school is for sure.
Prayerful with each new year I will grow.

College is the direction I think I will pursue.
A major and a minor
Is what I have chosen too.
Stacks of research papers
I know I must write.
Mostly work, no play, and no party life!
Whatever it takes to make it through.

Beyond the Woes of Me!

Here's to the future!
Cheers to my past!
I have lovely thoughts and great memories
That will always last.

I'll hold on to the memories.
So, goodbye, high school!

New Beginnings

Thirteen long years
Of education have passed.
You've finally reached the top.
However, it's only the beginning,
So, don't you ever stop!
Keep reaching for life's fulfillment,
By trying to reach your goals.
Fulfilling your destiny,
With precious memories to hold.

Classmates, as you move
Along your journey,
Don't forget to look back
Every now and then.
Laughing at things in the past,
Or just the relationship
With a special friend.

Beyond the Woes of Me!

Start thinking of your future,
For this is a new start.
Share moments with someone special.
Share portions of your heart.

Be loving, kind, and gentle.
Be ambitious, true, and fair.
While loving you, yes be free.
Show that someone special that you care.

School is out for us all.
It's time for the fun.
I know that I can say this much:
I've only just begun!

We are starting a new journey.
We are pursuing our future goals.
We are moving in different directions,
As we travel along life's road.

Epitaph—What's Left Inside of Me?

We've enjoyed your stay
While here on earth.
Your face we've often cherished.

We've loved you in so many ways.
I believe you're with God,
And your soul didn't perish.

I loved you so, for many reasons.
I know you felt the same.

When you died, I felt so lonely.
It was myself I often blamed.

Beyond the Woes of Me!

I am happy that you are free right now.
You've left this world of sin.

So, go and sing with the angels in Paradise,
The place they call Heaven.
I really loved to hear you sing,
Especially when you sang to me.

I want you to know I love you still,
For with you gone,
All I have are memories.

Myself

Sitting here and reflecting,
How do I talk about myself?
Thinking of the many times,
When I put pride upon the shelf.

I guess I'll say I am lovable.
I guess I'll say I am fun.
When it comes to being self-reliant,
Oh, yes, I am the one.

Some people say I'm nice,
And others say I'm sweet.
I'm glad to be made in the image of God.
Oh, yes, that makes me unique.

Oh, for there is but one me.
There is none other to compare.

Beyond the Woes of Me!

A self-less heart, one so giving;
A sacrificed life thus shared.

A love for family, inclusive, and extended,
My friends are all loved too.
The greatest love that I have found
Is loving no one other than WHOM?

My Thoughts

Sometimes I sit and wonder,
About many things.
Why the world has so many problems,
And how does a bird sing?

What is this thing called "life" all about?
Why are some people happy,
And so many sad?
Why do good people suffer
From decisions made by those who are bad?

Sometimes I sit and wonder
Why is the world this way?
I wonder about an awesome God
That took time to separate night from day.

Beyond the Woes of Me!

The various shades of color,
Yes, many of the skin.
The textures of the hair,
Down to the shapes of the
Lips, hips, and chin.
My thoughts are varied
And cover a myriad of topics too:
The economy, politics, and world issues,
Just to name a few.

I am so blessed to think about God
And to say:

*"How precious to me are
your thoughts, God!
How vast is the sum of them!"*
— Psalm 139:17

The Sparrow and Me

Well, what about a thought?
Peace, what a feeling!
Ever so wonderful!
And, yes, oh so great!

Just like a sparrow,
When he glides through the sky.
Not a care in the world does he have.

Imagine the flight of the sparrow
As he feels the wind
While soaring through the
Heights of the sky.

Let the inner being be at rest
Let it be free.

Beyond the Woes of Me!

Let not the cares of this world keep thee
In wonder or worry of life's uncertainties.

Just as the sparrow worries not
About the portrayal of what it is
Or it should be.
Its focus is flying high,
Just being free.

Let us, the human,
Enjoy who we are.
Let us enjoy being free.
To be free, to be me,
It is great!

To glide from one destination
To the next in life
Feels, oh, so great!
Liberty is so sweet,
So real to me.

The Sparrow and Me

The inner being daily is
Greatly enhanced by the Spirit.
My God, in Whom I trust,
Takes care of the sparrow.
Will He not take care of me?

The wings of a sparrow, as they open,
Extend from the east to the west.
The flight it has begun.
As the sky is his limit,
How much more do we have,
As we are known as God's sons?

The beak of the sparrow,
As he eats his prey,
Has no respective crumb
That will not satisfy his hunger.

Does he worry of what he shall eat?
No not the sparrow.
For God watches over the sparrow,
And, oh yes, He watches over me.

Beyond the Woes of Me!

The eye of the sparrow,
Though small it may seem,
Enables the sight
Of those yet to be claimed.
The instinct of what is yet to come
Does not bother the sparrow.
Why? God's eye is on the sparrow.
And, oh yes, I know He watches me.

So, if the sparrow, as small as one may be,
Can worry of nothing, travels freely,
Eats freely, sleeps freely,
And enjoys the limitless sky.

The sparrow doesn't worry
Of who, what, when, where, how, or why.
Reason—God's eye is on the sparrow,
And so I know He watches me.

Am I not more of God's image
Than the sparrow?

The Sparrow and Me

Does not God care more
For me than this sparrow?

Why be it, then, man should sit
And worry about the things in life?
When it is God whose eye is on the sparrow.
And, oh yes, I know He watches over me.

Praise be to God!

Scriptures on WHO THE WORD SAYS I AM

I praise you because I am
fearfully and wonderfully made;
your works are wonderful;
I know that full well.
— Psalm 139:14

Everyone who believes that
Jesus is the Christ is born of
God, and everyone who loves the
father loves his child as well.
— 1 John 5:1

Blessed are the peacemakers,
for they will be called children of God.
— Matthew 5:9

For those who are led by the Spirit
of God are the children of God.
— Romans 8:14

Your Notes

Section 4

Finding God

As I began to search the Scriptures to find out what the Word says I am, I found that many things I believed were quite the contrary to what God says about me. Below are a few points I would like to share. The Lord would like to remind all of us who are considered to be His children:

We are created in His Image.

So, God created mankind in his own image, in the image of God he created them; male and female he created them.
— Genesis 1:27

We are saved by His grace.

For it is by grace you have been saved, through faith—and this is not from yourselves, it is the gift of God—not by works, so that not one can boast.
— Ephesians 2:8-9

The LORD is my strength and my defense;
he has become my salvation
— Exodus 15:2

We can be like Christ.

Therefore, if you have any
encouragement from being united with
Christ, if any comfort from his love,
if any common sharing in the Spirit,
if any tenderness and compassion,
then make my joy complete by being
like-minded, having the same love,
being one in spirit and of one mind.
— Philippians 2:1-2

Because of Jesus, we are healed.

But he was pierced for our transgressions,
he was crushed for our iniquities:
the punishment that brought

us peace was on him,
and by his wounds we are healed.
— Isaiah 53:5

We are chosen.

But you are a chosen people, a royal
priesthood, a holy nation, God's special
possession, that you may declare the
praises of him who called you out of
darkness into his wonderful light.
— 1 Peter 2:9

We are conquerors.

No, in all these things we are more
than conquerors through him who
loved us. For I am convinced that
neither death nor life, neither angels
nor demons, neither the present nor
the future, nor any power, neither
height nor depth, nor anything

70

*else in all creation, will be able to
separate us from the love of God
that is in Christ Jesus our Lord.*
— Romans 8:37-39

We have the victory.

*Now this I know:
The LORD gives victory to his anointed.
He answers him from his
heavenly sanctuary
with the victorious power
of his right hand.*
— Psalm 20:6

We each will have our season.

*There is a time for everything,
and a season for every activity
under the heavens:
a time to be born and a time to die,
a time to plant and a time to uproot,*

Beyond the Woes of Me!

a time to kill and a time to heal,
a time to tear down and a time to build,
a time to weep and a time to laugh,
a time to mourn and a time to dance,
a time to scatter stones and
a time to gather them,
a time to embrace and
a time to refrain from embracing,
a time to search and a time to give up,
a time to keep and a time to throw away,
a time to tear and a time to mend,
a time to be silent and a time to speak,
a time to love and a time to hate,
a time for war and a time for peace.
— Ecclesiastes 3:1-8

Your Notes

Dear Momma

Sometimes I feel like a black
rose in a dozen of red.
I lay down, and when I wake,
I wish to be in my bed.
I feel as if I was kidnapped while
in tha middle of a nap.

I don't know exactly how to
express what I feel.
So, my baby told me to just be real.
But, she don't understand the deal.
Since day one, I was real, and
if not I should be killed.

Cause in my eyes I was forced on change.
But in their eyes, it's just a different range.
Now ain't that strange?

Dear Momma

I've been moved around
like a bike tied by chains.
Even though they say "it's in my brains."

You may say, "What is he talkin bout?"
But you don't understand, how
bad I want to be in tha South.
Cause it's like I've been torn away.
Even though in my heart is where y'all stay.

He may say he's goin to make me
stay; until that day in May.
I can't wait until that late December day.
Because, you see, on that day,
I'll be on my merry little way.

Yeah, and in New Orleans is
where I'm goin to STAY!

I LOVE YOU!

Eric

In Closing

Throughout life, we will have ups and downs, highs and lows. I have penned the words in this book to inspire, to encourage, and to give HOPE to others. Through it all, I have learned to put my trust in God.

He that dwelleth in the secret place of the most High shall abide under the shadow of the Almighty. I will say of the Lord, He is my refuge and my fortress: my God; in him will I trust.
— Psalm 91:1-2

Cast all your anxiety on him because he cares for you.
— 1 Peter 5:7

About the Author

Dr. Dawn Greay is not just an educator by profession; she is also a prophetic psalmist in ministry. An ordained elder, she is willing to go forth and do what God has called her to do: spread His love and share HOPE with all who dare to read these pages.

Author Contact Page

For Speaking Engagements,
please contact Dr. Dawn Greay at:

dgodsen685@gmail.com

or

225.283.1006